GAUDÍ

an introduction to his architecture

Text
JUAN-EDUARDO CIRLOT
Photography
PERE VIVAS / RICARD PLA

TRIANGLE ▼ POSTALS

CASA VICENS

EL CAPRICHO

GÜELL PAVILIONS

GÜELL PALACE

THERESAN COLLEGE

EPISCOPAL PALACE

CASA BOTINES

GÜELL BODEGAS

CASA CALVET

BELLESGUARD

PARK GÜELL

CATHEDRAL OF MAJORCA

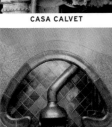

CASA BATLLÓ

LA PEDRERA

GÜELL CRYPT

SAGRADA FAMÍLIA

INTRODUCTION TO GAUDÍ'S ARCHITECTURE

There is a shroud of mystery surrounding Gaudí. In all probability, the first mist preventing us from gaining access to his work is the intrinsic mysteriousness of all genius and, at the end of the day, of all human spirit. The situation is complicated by the well-known fact that Gaudí wished to create an aura of silence around his persona, while, at the same time as maintaining this secretiveness – in other words, the annihilation of his fundamental values – gave expression and symbolisation to his moods and incredible mental power. Gaudí, despite his closeness to us in terms of time, rises before us surrounded by the revered magic which Jung called the *manna* personality. He is the wise man, the enlightened doctor – a trait that draws him close to Ramon Llull, another mysterious Catalan lost in the mists of time since the 13th century –; he is the artist whose superiority not only stems from both intellectual and spiritual possibilities but which sprouts, as a way of describing it, from the total and whole transformation of what he did and who he was. However, the second shroud of mystery lies in his particular era. Indeed, although close in time, his work was more a culmination of the long process that began with the rise of Christianity and pre-Romanesque art than the beginnings of our own times. And this, despite the fact that Gaudí's work, as an authentic creation of genius, or in other words, that which *generates*, gave us the rules and premonitions for a new concept in art, morphology and *pathos*.

←
PORTRAIT OF ANTONI
GAUDÍ AGED 26

One thing, however, are these shapes rising from the heart of his work and another very distinct factor is the whole of this work as an expression of a period. The serious caesura that separates the Modernist period from ours could be explained by stylistic, social or political traits. Modernist art can be discovered in the shaping of the 19th century and appears indistinct in the work of some painters, especially that of Cézanne (1839-1906). We will say only one thing. The Modernist period still belonged, to a great extent, to the cultural eclecticism of the second half of the 19th century, based on admitting multiplicity and complexity, in short, that which is aged. In contrast, our era comes from a youthful demand, of a break with the past, of the reconquest of a new simplicity, of the rejection of the complex, to a more or lesser extent. The mere contemplation of Gaudí's works, despite the profound inner and obvious links that join them, despite their unique expression of a particular era, tests this multiplicity and complexity that our feelings about the world want to reject. We say want because in this word there coexists, despite everything, a certain juxtaposition of distinct but nevertheless contradictory elements: functionalism and organic architecture and abstract painting and informal use of matter, non-figurative ascesis and surreal Baroque. The perceptible differences in Gaudí's creative work are undoubtedly due to perfectly justified distinct factors: the siting of the work and the objective respect the architect has for local peculiarities and technical traditions. It has been clearly observed that outside Catalonia he never used this a la Catalan brick vaulting, which are a precedent for current shells of buildings. Gaudí's work is also influenced by different eras: the Mudejar style of the earlier period and expressive morphology in the golden age of the Casa Milà, the Park Güell and the crypt of the church of the Colònia Güell. Nevertheless, at the same time, there is an intrinsic and I would dare to say "sacred monstrosity" in the variety of Gaudí's work that we would never find in Gropius or Moore, nor in the architects and artists who are recognised as having the most ability in variation and even contradiction, such as Frank Lloyd Wright or Picasso. This is because Gaudí's diversity does not lie in merely intellectual or instinctive terrain. The central point of the mystery of Gaudí's personality resides precisely in this innate ability to discover, reveal and recreate *an entire universe*. More than for reasons of his destiny or the influences of his upbringing, which must have brought him close to God enough to turn him into a mystical and pious person, it must have been the living discovery – compensated by his deep humility – of the divine factor that resided in his inner self. His own magnificent ability for invention that filled him with pleasure must have pushed him towards that Divinity with which he felt connected to the innermost depths of his whole being.

→
CARICATURE OF GAUDÍ
PUBLISHED IN
"LA PUBLICITAT"
ON 13TH OF JUNE 1926

IDEOLOGICAL ELEMENTS OF HIS TIME

We have certainly not combed Gaudí's reading – who would be able to? – or even his travels. Nevertheless, on the other hand, we are sure that the explanation we seek could not be found in such sources. It has been seen that brilliant people, as yet another factor of their authority, have an incredible informative speed. This ability enabled Balzac, for example, to describe thousands of places and situations he saw without realising it with a "capacity of register" inaccessible to the majority of human beings. The ideological elements that "existed" in Gaudí's time must have been captured, deepened and analysed unconsciously and subliminally, continuously and profoundly effectively. Some of these elements have been described. For example, from his known studies, that of the theoretical works of Viollet-le-Duc (1814-1879), or the contact he kept with his favourite teachers: Francesc Llorens i Barba (1820-1872), who taught him philosophy and literature; and Pablo Milà i Fontanals (1810-1883), with whom he studied the theory and history of art. The latter's concepts and ideas are well known, based on integrating art into culture, thus breaking the isolation of artistic acts in order to incorporate them into daily life, a tendency which Gaudí had no option but be interested in. Regarding Llorens i Barba, we know that he preached a spiritualist doctrine, in which philosophy was not a specialisation but a piece of "complete knowledge". Some of this thinker's ideas are nearly enough to explain part of Gaudí's ideology: an ideology unformulated in written terms but patent and active in his architectural-expressive creativity. It is hard to believe,

←
SIFFOT DESIGNED BY GAUDÍ
WHEN FONTSERÉ'S ASSISTANT,
IN CIUTADELLA PARK

but for Llorens i Barba, "philosophical belief" was a *dark and subjective state*, a mystical doctrine if there is one. He believed, alternatively, in the "activity of substances subject to the first cause". And with this he approached, but without accepting everything that it involved, the monism of Ernst Haeckel, whose ideas and investigations "floated" around the air in Gaudí's formative years. Haeckel (1834-1919) fought for a biological conception of the universe in which matter was integrated, not in life, but in thought, a theory that Teilhard de Chardin, later on, often endorsed in part. On the other hand, Haeckel published many studies about natural forms (protozoans, radiolarians, medusas, etc.). When Folguera tells us that Gaudí, as well as history, studied "nature", we should suppose that he would have been interested in the most representative works of his time, in which the morphological obsession of pre-modernism had an abundant and nutritious grazing land. Between 1860 and 1890, Haeckel published numerous books of the morphology of natural beings, some of which were translated into Spanish, such as the *General Morphology of Organisms* (Barcelona, 1887). In our opinion, Gaudí's work shows an advance from traditional architecture towards new architectural structures based on mechanics and experiments such as the catenaries but, at the same time, and through the medieval and oriental tendencies in style, *openly enters the world of natural morphology which does not copy but transforms and integrates it into an architectural or structural-ornamental factor*. The colour used in his polychrome often reminds one more of the underwater flora and fauna than of the natural elements that could normally be seen. The rounding off of the bell towers of the

→
ILLUSTRATIONS FROM
THE "GENERAL MORPHOLOGY
OF THE ORGANISMS" BY
ERNST HAECKEL

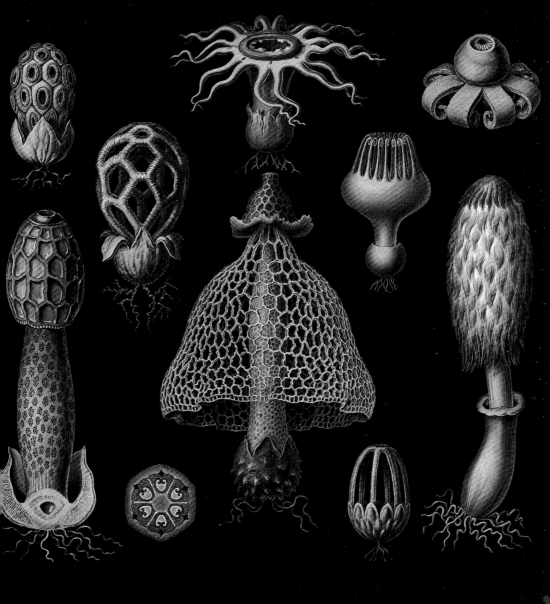

Sagrada Família possess the qualities and drive of the medusa before that of the flower, and structures of radiolarian were clearly used by Gaudí on specific details, such as the peep-holes of the Casa Calvet. There is no doubt, and this backs up what we have said of Gaudí's intrinsic complexity, that other very distinct ideological currents converge in his thought. This explains the spiritualist tendency, which had its roots in Celtic culture, the English Pre-Raphaelite doctrine (the Pre-Raphaelite Brotherhood was founded in 1848) and which, through the "Art and Crafts" movement of William Morris in 1861, rekindled by Ashbee in 1888, and the architects and decorators of the Glasgow School, reached Catalonia con-tinuously to have a long-lasting influence. However, what could have been a dramatic ide-ological factor in Gaudí's time could be approached in other terms. If we were to refer to literature, we would see that through the naturalism of Zola (1840-1902) or by penetrat-ing the cosmic symbolism of Melville (1819-1891) and the "willingness of power" of Nietzsche (1844-1900) it could be, in some way or another, transformed and "saved" by a mystic tendency. A Nietzsche redeemed by Parsifal, with the gaze fixed on the "Wild Mountain" or on the Montsalvat (or on Montserrat), could be very close to, as regards the general tone of the personality, the example of a Gaudí work. It must be emphasised in say-ing this, however, that we do not wish to do anything more than draw co-ordinates around the deeply unyielding figure of the great Catalan architect. A factor that should also not be

←
FACADE OF THE NATIVITY
ON THE SAGRADA FAMÍLIA
UNDER CONSTRUCTION

underestimated in considering the ideological "façades" of a Gaudí piece is the repressed and intrinsically contradictory personality of the author of the Sagrada Família. The complexity of his work, which to a large extent resides in his time (still placed in nineteenth-century eclecticism, as we say), is also rooted in such contradictions or, in other words, divergent impulses. Sometimes they are miraculously combined – and then the works of the artist arise in a purer and more unitary form – but sometimes they juxtapose each other and we are witness to this kind of struggle on the seabed that certain Gaudí creations often evoke. Traditionalism and modernism, love for everything "Mediterranean" and brusque immersions to hinterlands that might be either Germanic or African (this African influence is strange by three men from Reus: Prim (1814-1870), winner of the Battle of Castillejos in 1860; Fortuny (1838-1874), painter of Moroccan themes and of Prim's heroic feat; and Gaudí, creator, with the project of the building for the Catholic Missions of Tangier. This construction had an unmistakable relationship – strangely and inexplicably – with the Hamite constructions of Togo and Kreis Següela). Added to that was refinement, almost worshipful of childish myths and a dream-like atmosphere, such as the pavilions in Park Güell. Also present was a tense surliness that was tremendously virile and dramatic, such as the tawny porticoes of leaning columns in the above-mentioned park. We also find the calculating tendency, of "seeing the pressure lines" contrasted with pure imagination and his functional intuitions upsetting the expressionism. Nevertheless, the joining of opposites often resolves antinomies and this tendency towards mechanical expression seems to us to be more than an expression of a cold "technical" side to Gaudí, rather his faith in *everything* that was beautiful and divinely demonstrated. Furthermore, if in the contradictions of the great architect, there was a tendency that he could dominate, it was that of spiritualism. We have irrefutable evidence of this in Gaudí's own evolution, increasingly immersed in the calling that was plainly evident in his Sagrada Família work. Needless to say, therefore, in summing up, that the aesthetic ideology of Gaudí coincides with Schoenberg's thesis "to put into practice a scientific principle up to the final consequences". This is emphasised if we add that the "scientific principle" appears as a profane side of a revelation that was originally superior and extraordinarily mundane in its nature. Even in the radiolarians Gaudí saw God, as he did in the strength lines and the funicular polygons. The fact that he preferred the helicoid and parabola to the circle, triangle and square and to Plato's sphere is the fact that shows precisely the "difference" between classical culture and modernist *pathos* and the tearing apart of a tradition, resulting in mutation and the origin of a new world for mankind.

→
FUNGIFORM CUPOLA
OF ONE OF THE PAVILIONS
IN PARK GÜELL
→
PEEPHOLE ON THE DOOR
OF THE CASA CALVET

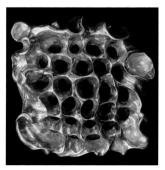

THE EARLY WORKS (1878-1892)

Gaudí's early period is distinguished by the Mudejar influence, for alternating between this orientalist suggestion and medievalist emphasis, and for the progressive and growing appearance of the elements that correspond to Gaudí's mature period. Despite that nevertheless it can be seen in his works that Gaudí put into practice two of his concepts that it is important to describe. When he was 26, Gaudí wrote in a diary, "The ornamentation has been, is and will be coloured. Nature does not produce anything that is monochrome or uniform in colour: neither vegetation nor in geology, nor in topography nor in the animal kingdom. The contrast in colour is always more or less alive and from this we are obliged to colour in part or all of an architectural piece, colouring that will perhaps disappear when the hand of time gives it another colour that is more befitting and precise for something old". Besides the total demonstration in favour of colour in architecture, what is really interesting in this statement is that Gaudí conceived architecture *within* nature, loyal to all its laws, even the external ones, that architecture always violated nature with its structures, it seems. The statement relating to colouring due to the "hand of time" is also important in that it corroborates, as if it were necessary to do so, the architect's sensitivity to colour-texture, to the qualities of the material. Another valuable feature of Gaudí is one described by Rubió who transcribed Gaudí saying that

his greatest quality consisted in "knowing exactly whether something had to be higher or lower, flatter or more curved. This is nothing more than a quality for clairvoyance and I, luckily, can see it". He added, "I cannot do anything about it. I just thank God and that is it". One can see an intuitive Gaudí here, who would use the mechanics to broaden his domain, but who "knew" the shape, as did the great sculptors-architects of the past. What Gaudí did not know was the *intensity* of this gift of knowing if "something had to be higher or lower, flatter or more curved", an intensity that helped him discover that the "interesting" shapes are not flat ones but concave or convex ones. This discovery was, nevertheless, made gradually and the works covering his early period are dominated by flat surfaces and traditional formulas enriched by decorative additions or also by the typical Gaudí structures such as the parabolic arches in the Casa Vicens (1883-1888). Here the glazed ceramic tile and wrought iron contribute to creating a vision of beauty. As regards the general structure of the building, Gaudí managed to enliven it by using all the resources found in the brick, a rich ground plan in angles and surfaces covered with strips of glazed ceramic tiles in relief. The grille with very naturalistic iron palms possesses a particular strength, so characteristic of Gaudí's work.

The project for the "Obrera Mataronense", of which only the stonework was ever completed, shows the casing of the stairway, in brick, on the exterior of the building and attached to it. This solution, in another stylistic sphere, would be taken up by Gropius in 1914 for his Werkbund factory in Cologne. Between 1883-1885, Gaudí built the "El Capricho" estate in Comillas (Santander), a work that maintained the tendencies shown in the Casa Vicens, but this time with more dramatic strength. The ornamentation on the tower that rises over the entrance portico is of a character that is simultaneously both "technical" and regressive and the geometry of the dome covering it possesses a quite violent intensity. It is an authentic work of cubism produced a full quarter of a century in advance and which clearly has the stamp of Gaudí's personality as a great master which does not bow to the more decadent and timid dictates of what we could call "orthodox modernism". In 1883, Gaudí, on accepting the appointment of architect of the Sagrada Família (Joan Martorell, architectural author of the Francisco de Paula del Villar project having turned the appointment down), acquired a responsibility that would end up identified with his destiny and absorbing all his creative energies when, from the outbreak of the first world war in 1914, he abandoned all profane work. Between 1884-1888, Gaudí worked intensively for Eusebi Güell, the illustrious figure he had first met in 1878 and

→
DRAWING OF THE
PROJECT FOR THE
MATARÓ WORKERS'
HOUSING ESTATE

who was to be his main client and patron. For Güell he built the palatial house in Nou de la Rambla Street, where he used funicular arches at the entrances and where he structured spaces of great monumental dimensions and strange articulations that are very close to, or even anticipate, some of those by Behrens. In this work Gaudí appears as the inventor of decorative or architectural elements conceived as sculptures, both in the wrought iron grilles of the entrance and in the geometrical chimneys that provide a pronounced magical air to the building's flat roof. Already appearing in these chimneys is the characteristic covering of pieces of glazed ceramic tile creating abstract compositions. Gaudí also designed the furnishing as he had done in the Casa Vicens. He also built the Pedralbes pavilions for Güell, highlighted by the value of the wrought ironwork with the "Dragon", which could, in all honesty, be considered as the direct ancestor of all the iron sculpture that was produced so much during the twentieth century, starting from the works of Gargallo and González.

This early period also corresponds to several important buildings in which the artistic and personal influence of Gaudí is still not shown with the invasive strength of the following period. Between 1888-1890 he built the Theresan college in Ganduxer Street, Barcelona, with monumental faces of brick rhymed by parabolic arches and in which still persists a certain Mudejar style. Between 1889-1893 work began on the grand Episcopal Palace of Astorga (León) with its splayed portals, an austere construction in granite and which includes ceramic decoration on the second floor. 1891-1892 represents the building of the "Los Botines" in León, a work containing a naturalistic sculpture over the facade of St. George slaying the dragon. This is the first time we see Gaudí use, paradoxically, what he believed to be sculpture, in contrast to the great abstract sculpture represented by his architectural work in details and as a whole and without forgetting his own architectural values and technical advances. Parallel to these works, Gaudí worked on the Sagrada Família, firstly on the crypt (1884-1887), begun by Villar, and later on the apse, which maintains the neo-gothic style to a great extent and which rises to a height of fifty metres.

→→
BEGINNING OF THE
CONSTRUCTION OF
THE CRYPT AND APSE OF
THE TEMPLE OF
THE SAGRADA FAMÍLIA

CASA VICENS

The Casa Vicens was the first important work undertaken by Gaudí. Situated in Carrer Les Carolines, it was built between 1883 and 1888 at the behest of the ceramic tile manufacturer Manuel Vicens Montaner. The Mudejar style – much used by Barcelona architects of the time – is recreated and surpassed in this building in which the combination of the tiles and bricks is expressed with an extraordinary strength.

P. 28-29

←

GAUDÍ PAYS SPECIAL
ATTENTION TO THE ANGLES
OF THE BUILDING IN ORDER
TO AVOID STIFFNESS. IN THE
PHOTOGRAPH, A DETAIL OF
THE BALCONY

←

THE BUILDING IS COVERED
IN GEOMETRICALLY-SHAPED
CERAMICS. THE TILING WAS
DESIGNED BY GAUDÍ FOLLOWING
THE MODEL OF THE AFRICAN
MARIGOLDS (TAGETES PATULA)
WHICH GREW ON THE SITE

→

THE CAST IRON RAILING WAS
MADE FROM CLAY MODELS OF
THE PALM LEAVES THAT WERE
ON THE SITE

→

GAUDÍ CONCEIVED A TOTAL
DESIGN OF THE BUILDING
WHICH, AS WELL AS THE
METICULOUS CARE TAKEN
IN EACH EXTERIOR DETAIL,
INCLUDED THE INTERIOR DESIGN
WHICH IS HIGHLIGHTED BY THE
MURAL PAINTINGS AND
CABINETWORK

P. 32-33

→

ON THE CEILING OF THE FIRST
FLOOR, TORRES MASSANA
PAINTED A "TROMPE L'OEIL",
CREATING THE ILLUSION OF
A CONNECTION WITH THE
EXTERIOR

→

THE SMALL SMOKING ROOM
SHOWS THE ORIENTAL TASTE
OF THE PERIOD

EL CAPRICHO

Situated in the Santander village of Comillas and built between 1883 and 1885 for Máximo Díaz de Quijano, the holiday villa, "The treat", was overseen entirely by the architect Cristóbal Cascante Colom, who followed the instructions sent by Gaudí from Barcelona. The work, in which the tendencies of the Casa Vicens are maintained, but with more dramatic force, is the confirmation of Gaudí's personal modernism.

→
THE TOWER, SIMILAR TO
A MINARET, IS THE PART
THAT MOST DEFINES THIS
BUILDING AND IS THE FIRST
EXAMPLE OF AN
ARCHITECTURAL SOLUTION
THAT WOULD APPEAR IN
OTHER CONSTRUCTIONS
SUCH AS BELLESGUARD
OR THE PAVILIONS OF
PARK GÜELL
→
THE EXTERIOR OF THE
BUILDING IS CHARACTERISED
BY THE USE OF BRICKS
ADORNED WITH ROWS OF
GLAZED CERAMIC AND THE
SUPERIMPOSITION OF
THE CURVED SURFACE OVER
THE STRAIGHT ONE

GÜELL PAVILIONS

Between 1884 and 1887 Gaudí built the pavilions of the entrance and stables for the estate that the Güell family had in Les Corts. This work was the architect's first collaboration with Eusebi Güell, the Catalan businessman whose sponsorship would boost the architect's fame in a determinant way. From these pavilions, worth noting is the dragon doorway, a sculpture in cast iron designed by Gaudí himself and produced in the Barcelona workshop of Vallet and Piqué in 1885. This dragon was originally polychromed and came to life by means of an ingenious device.

P. 40-41
←
THE PAVILIONS ARE
EVOCATIVE OF MUDEJAR
ARCHITECTURE
REINTERPRETED THROUGH
GAUDÍ'S MODERNISM

→
THE GÜELL ESTATE REMINDS
ONE OF THE MYTHICAL
GARDEN OF HESPERIDES
WHERE HERCULES STOLE THE
GOLDEN FRUITS. THIS MYTH
WAS RECREATED IN
"L'ATLANTIDA" BY THE
CATALAN POET JACINT
VERDAGUER, A FREQUENT
VISITOR TO THE ESTATE. IN
THE PICTURE, THE ORANGE
TREE MADE WITH ANTIMONY
→
PARABOLIC ARCHES FROM
THE OLD STABLES WHICH
TODAY HOUSE THE GAUDÍ
CENTRE

→
THE USE OF INDUSTRIAL
ARTS SUCH AS CAST
IRONWORK WOULD BE ONE
OF THE MOST OUTSTANDING
ASPECTS OF GAUDIAN WORK
→
GAUDÍ PROVIDES A VISUAL
EXALTATION OF THE
FUNCTIONAL ROOFING
ELEMENTS SUCH AS
CHIMNEYS, CUPOLAS AND
VENTILATION DUCTS, ETC.

GÜELL PALACE

In the Carrer Nou de la Rambla stands this majestic palace which Antoni Gaudí built between 1886 and 1888, for Eusebi Güell and Bacigalupi. Güell chose an unusual architect to erect not a house but a palace, which he would later show off to his acquaintances with concerts and exhibitions, etc. Gaudí's peculiarity expressed the new language of the bourgeoisie, created deliberately to tell a new history in which the patron had a key role. This palace, a rising metaphor, like Güell, extends from the dark basement of poverty to the festival of colour at the top culminating in the golden sunlight of wealth.

P. 48-49
←
IN ALL THE PALACE, GAUDÍ
USED FINE MATERIALS. IN
THE PICTURE, THE MARBLE
STAIRWAY IN THE MAIN
ENTRANCE
←
THE USE OF CAST IRON
GENERATES THE APPEARANCE
OF SUGGESTIVE TEXTURES

→
THE BASEMENT STABLES WERE
BUILT FROM THICK BRICK
COLUMNS WITH FUNGIFORM
CAPITALS

→
THE COFFERED CEILING
IS ALSO A SOLID SUPPORT
STRUCTURE
→
THE CUPOLA IS MADE UP
OF PERFORATED HEXAGONAL
PIECES THAT ALLOW THE
LIGHT TO ENTER IN SUCH
A WAY AS TO IMITATE A
CELESTIAL VAULT THROUGH
WHICH THE STARS SHINE
BRIGHTLY

P. 54-55
→
DETAIL OF THE PARABOLIC
ARCHES
→
DESPITE THE COMPLEX
ARCHITECTURAL STRUCTURE
OF THE GÜELL PALACE, THE
INTERIOR SPACES ARE
FLOWING

P. 56-57
→
THE CHIMNEY TOPS WERE
RESTORED IN 1994 BY
DIFFERENT PLASTIC ARTISTS
→
ON THE ROOF A SERIES
OF TWENTY SCULPTURAL
CHIMNEYS SURROUND THE
SKYLIGHT ON THE CENTRAL
SALON

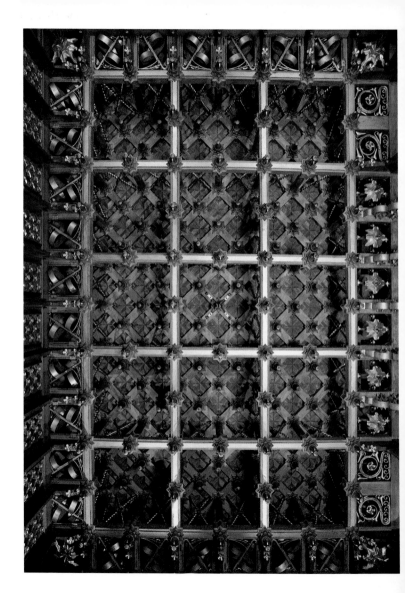

THERESAN COLLEGE

The building was constructed between 1888 and 1890 at the behest of Enric d'Ossó, the founding priest of the congregation of Theresan nuns. In contrast with other works, Gaudí was subject to strict economic controls. This condition explains the sober appearance of the college in which the architect uses a rational and severe language where the Mudejar style persists.

P. 60-61

←
THE BUILDING'S EXTERIOR
AUSTERITY CONTRASTS WITH
THE WARM ATMOSPHERE
ATTAINED IN THE INTERIOR
THANKS TO THE MAGNIFICENT
DISTRIBUTION OF LIGHT

→
IN A LETTER TO THE MOTHER
SUPERIOR, OSSÓ DESCRIBED
THE BUILDING IN THE
FOLLOWING WAY: "THE
COLLEGE WILL BE ADORNED
WITH DECORATION AND
UNUSUAL AND UNIQUE IN
THE STYLE OF GAUDÍ"
  →
DOOR OF THE MAIN ENTRANCE
WITH THE HEART STABBED
WITH PAIN, A THERESAN
SYMBOL

EPISCOPAL PALACE
OF ASTORGA

In 1887, Joan Baptista Grau, the bishop of Astorga, entrusted Antoni Gaudí, his friend and countryman, with the construction of the Episcopal palace. The architect, who worked on this building from 1889 until 1893, abandoned the work after the death of the bishop, its main champion.

Gaudí worked out the project for the palace from books and photographs of León-style architecture and he used local building materials, such as chalk and granite from the Bierzo region. Nevertheless, the building shows the inappropriate and suggestive Gothic style of a fairytale castle.

CASA BOTINES

The Fernández-Andrés company, the successor to Homs & Botinás (the surname which when Hispanicized, comes out as "botines" with which the building is known), entrusted to Gaudí, through Eusebi Güell, the construction of a house in León. The building, on which work began in 1892, was erected in just ten months. In the lintel of the door, the Catalan architect placed a naturalist sculpture of St. George slaying the dragon.

Misiones Católicas de África

Tanger

THE PERIOD OF MATURITY (1892-1914)

All classifications by period are arbitrary and conventional: this has been repeated *ad nau-seam* and if, on the one hand, it were never repeated again, on the other, one could still never escape from these classifications even though pointing out their relativity. Gaudí had a special gift reserved only for the great creative artists – something that can be seen from studying biographies and artistic careers in detail –, his inventive power increasing uninterruptedly almost until the end of this life. In 1892, when he was forty, he began to show signs of a particular originality ("returning to the origin" according to Gaudí himself) which can only be judged as abrupt and revolutionary. The building project for the Catholic Missions in Tangier, with its seven central cones, apart from being connected to the African works we mentioned before, constructs a "cosmic image" or, in other words, a symbolic "model" of universal totality. This aspiration, within Gaudí's morphological inventions and technical experimentation, stayed with him in his inner self, later to appear in his projects for the church of the Colònia Güell and in his triumphal image of the Expiatory Temple of the Sagrada Família. The cone, or the parabolic or spindly tower, is the essential expressive element of this conception, along with the ground plan distribution of the whole that symbolically defines the idea of totality (centre surrounded by a series of four or seven elements). But while Gaudí advances along the path of his inventive creativity his personality is transformed and if his religiousness is confirmed, his disinterest in the external increases and his biographers,

←
PROJECT FOR THE
CATHOLIC MISSIONS
OF TANGIERS

or those that still remember him, can test the contrast between the young Gaudí who was almost a dandy and the mature Gaudí, indifferent to getting dressed or to his living conditions, his relationships with others and all that goes with it. Above all, from the death of his father in 1906, and in the last twenty years of his life, he threw himself into his work and thought so much that he forgot that he still had a body and lived in a material world inhabited by fellow beings, but similar only on the outside.

Gaudí's mysticism, however, never abandons the sensual, even glorious evaluation of natural morphology despite his abandonment of himself. Without sharing Haeckel's monism, mentioned before, we are nevertheless reminded of him and specifically, his conception of the world of which it has been said, "aproximated organic and inorganic nature, science and religion, thought and the material world", almost finally identifying the physical and the psychic. Gaudí's intensity sometimes appears to produce a similar result, but in Gaudí's ideology there was, we know, a perfect submission to orthodoxy. In this way, the expressions are more unconscious, symbolic and even repressed (like Beethoven's cordiality). After the Casa Calvet (1898-1900), a work with lively personal accents within general containment, comes the insistence on the neo-gothic of Bellesguard, with vaulting a la Catalan and the inspired use of the grille (1900-1909). We must now refer to Gaudí's two main collaborators, whose contribution should in no way be ignored. Francesc Berenguer (1866-1914), as can be seen from his Garraf work, despite not having an architectural qualification, was able to help him main-

→
DOOR OF THE MIRALLES
ESTATE (1902)

ly, perhaps, in the structural or mechanical side. On the other hand, Josep M. Jujol (1879-1949), "architectural painter", had an important role in the decoration of some exteriors and interiors, such as that of the Casa Batlló, in Passeig de Gràcia, Barcelona (1904-1907), the facade of which reminds one of Monet's *Water Lilies*, with their irregularly distributed discs, their deformed colourings of the flat surfaces (violets, lilacs, blues and greens), their marvellous chimneys, the sculptural forms, Moore-like by now, of the flat roof apron or the interior, etc. It is perhaps in this period when the modernist aspect of Gaudí's work really stands out the most, justifying the inclusion, though out of place, of the great master in the movement and of which Pevsner, knowing what we know, said in *Pioneers of Modern Design*, "Gaudí is the most significant artist of Art Nouveau... the only genius that this movement has really produced".

In the extremely important works described below, Gaudí's formal inventiveness is shown very clearly as is its transformation in expressive values of any structure. The flat surface, on being deformed, on warping, acquires values related to ovoid shapes and in this way anticipates the sculpture of Arp, Brancusi, Moore or Pevsner. The formal sections of these elements or the schemes that make up flat forms, such as the glass doors in the Casa Milà (1906-1912), provide the forms that would be abundant in the art of Arp, Miró or Calder. Gaudí conceives the architectural work as a living reality that he had to be able to "touch", as a manner of speaking, with his hands and really shape it. One is reminded of the craftsman-like sculpting ability of his elders which he transformed, magnified and integrated into his art, and there is room for a miraculous intuitiveness of what would reign in the art world over the next fifty years, produced at a time when the fauves were the most "advanced" (the orientalist decorative style of Matisse) and in which Picasso began his pink period. For reasons of repression, Gaudí plunged his sensuality into the springs of his spirit and from there it gushed, converted into visions such as that of the attic and roofing of the Casa Milà, which defied all logic and demonstrated his interest in geodesic lines. If this building, with its seven stone folds, which seem as much like the structure of Montserrat as they do of the insane rhythms of Van Gogh, is something quite unusual and prodigious, then the apex breaks all boundaries. Added to that, there are the architectural technical innovations, such as the elimination of interior walls and circular corridors that underline the biomorphic nature of the whole, revitalising the geology of the other side which is further enlivened by the prodigiously dynamic wrought iron grilles on the balconies. These pre-dated not just the archaic works in iron of the years between 1925-1930, but also the informal metallic forms of Claire Falkenstein, who recognised this in a "Homage to Gaudí". Regarding the chimneys and hatchways of the roofing, the helicoid and undulating forms predominate, softened by the lyrical white nuances of the tiling. There are also perforated spaces such as those which years later would be present in the expressive work of Moore and Hepworth.

In 1898, Gaudí had begun his studies for the church of the Colònia Güell in Santa Coloma de Cervelló, studies which lasted for ten years. The crypt, which is the only con-

structed part, was built between 1908 and 1914, the year in which Gaudí decided his work on this building was finished due to external reasons. A hyperboloid roof, inclining columns whose direction follow that of the strength lines marked by the push of the land and the weight of the roof are the crypt's main features, along with the use of vaulting *a la Catalan* and the incorporation of star-shaped stained-glass windows and strangely beautiful ceramic elements. The building is possibly Gaudí's masterwork in terms of overcoming complexity and in its strangeness *per se*. In Gaudí the hyper-rational and the irrational combine, the calculator who attracted attention in his youth and the intuitive one who "saw" the "best form" of a perfectly independent *Gestalt Theory*. It is in this crypt where these two facets of Gaudí's thought are best integrated. On the one hand, the architectural subversion that manifests itself in the leaning columns and their somewhat disturbing ambiguous relationship with nature, and on the other hand, the architect achieves a clear serenity that both springs from the visibility of its mechanical conceptions and from the conscience of the rhythm with which the resulting forms are articulated by. This work is also profoundly traditional in the deepest sense of the word. It is opposed to both the arbitrary establishment of the new and rootless and to the pursuit of the old and routine or through a lack of creative imagination. The synthesis of ordered

articulation or of live and animated detail and the formal totality of the whole is extraordinary and it is almost impossible to put into words. Only with an attentive and sensitive contemplation of this crypt, in which the

HE RESURRECTION
F CHRIST, THE FIRST
YSTERY OF GLORY
N MONTSERRAT

principles and very best results of Gaudí's tectonics are concentrated, immersing oneself in its crystalline and organic atmosphere, and with its "power" of infinite unfolding, can we get near to the expression that Gaudí demonstrated in a unique way. Brick and coloured glass, geometry and "gestures" or impulses that materialise in the structures, ancestral religiousness and a "displaced" or "other" sense or the architectural image all combine and multiply amongst themselves. The synthesis of contradictions, the *coincidentia oppositorum* is now attained and, in consequence, the keen observer will find serenity mastering the tormented and order within the imaginative of this work, whose high church would perhaps have been, once again, the surpassing of the superior.

Simultaneously, between 1900 and 1914, above all between 1900 and 1903, Gaudí worked on the urbanisation of the Muntanya Pelada area, creating the Park Güell there, representing another outstanding aspect of his art. His expression here is undoubtedly freer and in the contradictory elements, instead of combining them, he uses contrast with great frequency. On the one hand, we have an almost child-like world of beauty with magical colours on the main steps and in the entrance halls with their prodigious roofing which are like the sublimation and sweetening of the scaled roof of the Casa Batlló. Firstly, there is the hypostyle hall with its Grecian style interpreted a little like Stravinsky interprets the pre-classical musicians and the embellished ceiling with collages made from fragments of glasses, bottles and dolls, which it has been said may be the work of Jujol. Then, in contrast, the violence of the stone porticoes with leaning columns, typical of Gaudí, with a rhythm of the snake of Evil, and the containing walls with tree-shaped columns which are continued in the abstract caryatids of the higher part of the park, with abrupt and pointed rocks. Later on we see the sinuous beauty of an undefined and infinite rhythm of the bench coated in broken glazed tiles, in abstract compositions, exactly coeval with Kandinsky's first abstract works. To sum up, the whole park, with its contradictory beauty and unique strength in the world, is an extraordinary spot where man's spirit truly breathes.

→→
DETAILS OF BROKEN
COLLAGES (CASA BATLLÓ
AND PARK GÜELL) WHERE
THE COLOURIST STYLE
OF JUJOL CAN BE
APPRECIATED

 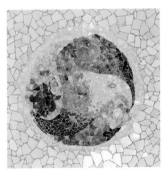

GÜELL BODEGAS

The Güell bodegas in Garraf, the coastal village between Barcelona and Sitges, were built between 1895 and 1901. Francesc Berenguer, Gaudí's assistant, was more than just a collaborator, but in fact the co-author of this building which, for some time, was attributed to him in its entirety.

→

THE EXTERIOR OF THE
BUILDING IS CONSTRUCTED
IN MASONRY OF GREY STONE
FROM THE GARRAF. THE SAME
MATERIAL WAS USED BY GAUDÍ
IN OTHER BUILDINGS IN
BARCELONA

→

EUSEBI GÜELL STORED A WINE
OF DUBIOUS QUALITY IN THE
GARRAF BODEGAS WHICH HE
EXPORTED TO CUBA IN THE
BOATS OF THE
TRANSATLANTIC COMPANY

CASA CALVET

Pere Mártir Calvet was the promoter of this property, which was built in Carrer Casp in Barcelona between 1898 and 1900. This time Gaudí recreated Catalan Baroque in this markedly nineteenth-century building. In 1900 the Casa Calvet won the prize which, for the first time, Barcelona City Council awarded to the best building.

The threshold of the door is framed by the letter "C" and the cypress tree, a symbol of welcome, on its upper part, and on both sides by two sewing mill looms which refer to the industrial activity of Calvet.

→
THE CASA CALVET IS A
BUILDING OF CARVED STONE
WHICH IS DOMINATED BY THE
CONTAINMENT. THE UPPER
CONTOUR IS UNDULATING AND
IS CROWNED WITH SPHERICAL
PINNACLES. THE ATTIC
BALCONIES ARE OF CAST AND
PERFORATED IRON PLATE,
PREFIGURING THOSE OF THE
CASA BATLLÓ
    →
FOR THE FIRST TIME, GAUDÍ
BUILDS A HOUSE FOR
SEVERAL DWELLERS. THE
FACADE CONTAINS MANY
SCULPTURAL DETAILS AMONG
WHICH FEATURE BUSTS OF
THE PATRON SAINTS OF
VILASSAR, THE BIRTHPLACE
OF CALVET, AND THE TWO
HORNS OF ABUNDANCE WHICH
CROWN THE DAIS, A
MYTHOLOGICAL OBJECT MUCH
USED AT THE TIME AS A
SYMBOL OF OPULENCE

→
IN THE FURNISHING OF THE
CASA CALVET GAUDÍ BEGAN
TO IMPRINT AN ORGANIC
CHARACTER INTO HIS DESIGN
→
ON THE DOORKNOCKER WE
COME ACROSS A CURIOUS
NATURALIST DETAIL: AN
INSECT THAT IS SQUASHED
BY A GREEK CROSS WHEN
KNOCKING AT THE DOOR

BELLESGUARD

At the beginning of the 15th century, Martín I the Humane built, at the foot of the Collserola hills, a palace which he called Bellesguard, meaning beautiful view. Five centuries later, in 1900, over the same spot, Antoni Gaudí erected a building for María Sagues Molins that demonstrated a peculiar neo-gothic style that pays homage to Catalan Gothic art and architecture.

→
DESPITE BEING INSPIRED BY
THE GOTHIC STYLE, GAUDÍ
SURPASSED MERE FORMAL
IMITATION
→
THE ROOFING OF
BELLESGUARD REMINDS ONE
OF A DRAGON'S HEAD

P. 92-93
→
DETAIL OF THE STAINED GLASS
IN THE MAIN DOOR
→
THE ROUGH APPEARANCE OF
THE SCHISTOSE STONE ON THE
EXTERIOR CONTRASTS WITH
THE WHITE LOBBY IN WHICH
LIGHT AND COLOUR FILTER
THROUGH THE STAINED GLASS

P. 94-95
→
THE STRUCTURE OF ARCHES
AND FALSE ARCHES ON THE
ATTICS DEMONSTRATES THE
FUSION OF FUNCTIONALITY
AND AESTHETICISM IN
GAUDIAN ARCHITECTURE

P. 96-97
→→
DETAIL OF THE ARCHES IN THE
SALON AND THE ATTIC

PARK GÜELL

On a piece of land on the Muntanya Pelada, in the Barcelona district of La Salut, Eusebi Güell wanted to build an urbanisation inspired by the concept of the garden city. In this he sought to return to nature, health and an escape from the insalubrious industrial city.

Mainly assisted by Rubió, Berenguer and Jujol, Gaudí worked on the construction of this park between 1900 and 1914, and even moved his home there in 1906.

BETWEEN 1900 AND 1903
THE MAIN BUILDINGS OF PARK
GÜELL WERE CONSTRUCTED:
WALLS, THE MAIN STAIRWAY,
PAVILIONS, ETC.
THE PAVILIONS STAND OUT
FOR THEIR IMAGINATIVE,
LYRICAL AND CHROMATIC
NATURE, AS WELL AS THE
EXPRESSIVENESS OF
ELEMENTS SUCH AS THE
TOWER CROWNED BY THE
FOUR-ARMED CROSS

→ THE CHIMNEYS IN THE FORM
OF A MUSHROOM – AMANITA
MUSCARIA – ARE AN
AESTHETIC AND SYMBOLIC
REFERENCE TRADITIONALLY
CONNECTED TO THE WORLD
OF MAGIC AND FAIRYTALES,
OF DRUIDS AND SHAMANS
AND OF GNOMES AND WITCHES

→
THE DORIC COLONNADE
WHICH SUPPORTS THE
SQUARE IS AN IMPOSING
SPACE THAT, PARADOXICALLY,
WAS DESIGNED AS A
MARKETPLACE

→
THE CEILING ROSES OF THE
COLONNADE, ATTRIBUTED
TO JUJOL, SHOW COLOURIST
INTERPRETATIONS OF SUNS,
MEDUSAS, ETC.

P. 110-111
←
THE CURVE IN MOVEMENT
AND THE SNAKING
UNDULATION DOMINATE THE
ARCHITECTURAL RHYTHM OF
PARK GÜELL, REACHING ITS
MAXIMUM EXPRESSION IN THE
SNAKE-LIKE BENCH AROUND
THE SQUARE

→→
THE BENCH IS DECORATED
WITH ABSTRACT
COMPOSITIONS COEVAL WITH
THE FIRST NON-FIGURATIVE
PAINTINGS OF KANDINSKY

P. 114-115
→
DETAILS OF THE BIOMORPHIC
DECORATION OF THE BENCH
→
PARK GÜELL HAS BEEN
COUNCIL-OWNED PROPERTY
SINCE 1922

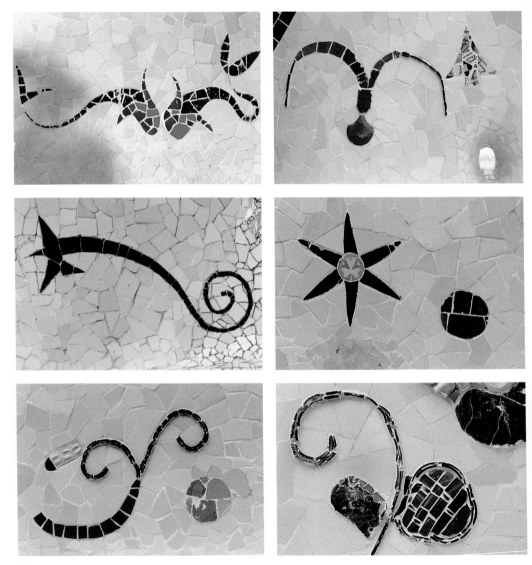

→
FRANCESC BERENGUER, ONE
OF GAUDÍ'S COLLABORATORS,
BUILT THIS HOUSE BETWEEN
1903 AND 1904 AS A MODEL
FOR THE CHALETS THAT WERE
TO BE BUILT IN PARK GÜELL.
GAUDÍ LIVED IN IT FROM 1906
AND TODAY IT IS THE MUSEUM
DEDICATED TO THE ARCHITECT

→
THE PORTICOES OF LEANING
COLUMNS CONTRAST THEIR
DRAMATIC TAWNY COLOUR
WITH THE CHROMATISM OF
THE REST OF THE PARK

CATHEDRAL OF MAJORCA

In 1901, Pere Campins Barceló, the bishop of Majorca, entrusted Gaudí to restore the cathedral. The works lasted for a total of ten years (1904-1914) and they were surrounded by constant controversy that resulted finally in Gaudí's dismissal after the death of Campins. Basically, the reform work involved recovering the space occupied by a Gothic-renaissance choir situated in the centre of the nave. Also collaborating on the restoration work were, among others, Joan Rubió Bellver, Vicente Villarrubias, Torres García and Josep Maria Jujol.

→
REPRESENTATION OF
BRANCHES AND EPISCOPAL
COATS OF ARMS
→
PAINTINGS BY JOSEP MARIA
JUJOL OVER THE CHOIR STALL

CASA BATLLÓ

Between 1904 and 1907, Antoni Gaudí worked for the industrialist Josep Batlló Casanovas reforming a house built in 1877 and located in Passeig de Gràcia in Barcelona. The decoration of the house, on which he was assisted by Josep Maria Jujol, expresses a fully-fledged modernist language. Nevertheless, the Barcelona population of the period were quite astonished by this work and quickly gave it nicknames such as the "house of bones" or the "house of yawns".

→
THE CASA BATLLÓ
REPRESENTS A NEW
ARCHITECTURAL EXPRESSION
IN WHICH REFERENCES TO
HISTORICAL STYLES HAVE
BEEN SURPASSED. THE FACADE
IS COVERED WITH CERAMIC
DISCS AND COLOURED GLASS
WINDOWS
   →
ON THE LOWER PART OF THE
MAIN FACADE, SANDSTONE
FROM MONTJUÏC WAS
SCULPTED INTO SINUOUS
FORMS

P. 126-127
→→
ENTRY STAIRWAY TO THE MAIN
FLOOR AND GENERAL
STAIRWAY OF THE BUILDING

P. 128-129
→
THE CHIMNEY IS AN EXAMPLE
OF THE PERFECT FUSION
BETWEEN DESIGN AND
FUNCTIONALITY

→
ON THE MAIN FLOOR, THE
DESIGN OF THE FURNISHING
AND CABINETWORK
DEMONSTRATE GAUDÍ'S
CONCERN FOR DETAIL.
THE GLASS PASTE DISCS
ON THE DOORS REMIND
ONE OF THE COLOURING
ON THE FACADE

P. 132-133
→
THE STRUCTURAL
HARMONY COMBINED WITH
THE AESTHETIC EFFECT
CREATE SUGGESTIVE
INTERIORS THAT ARE
FILLED WITH DETAIL.
THE DOORS ON THE MAIN
STAIRWAY ARE DECORATED
WITH CARVED SHAPES IN
RELIEF THAT ARE LIKE
BONES
    →
PARABOLIC ARCHES OF
THE ATTIC

→
THE BULBOUS CERAMIC THAT
SUPPORTS THE FOUR-ARMED
CROSS COMES FROM MAJORCA
 →
THE "SCALES" OF THE ROOF
ARE THE WORK OF PUJOL &
BAUCIS

P. 136-137
→→
ON THE ROOF, THE
SCULPTURAL TREATMENT OF
THE CHIMNEYS AND THEIR
COVERING WITH CERAMIC AND
PAINTED GLASS SHOW US
GAUDÍ AT HIS MOST
COLOURIST, PERHAPS DUE TO
HIS COLLABORATION WITH
JUJOL

LA PEDRERA

The widow Roser Segimon, heir to a vast fortune amassed by her first husband in the American colonies, was remarried to Pere Milà, an important Barcelona businessman. This wealthy couple wanted to build a building in Passeig de Gràcia and so they hired the most expensive and famous architect: Antoni Gaudí. The construction, which took from 1906 until 1912, resulted in a monumental building, but also caused disagreements between Gaudí and the Milà family. The Casa Milà was the architect's last piece of civil engineering.

→
GALLERY ON THE FIRST FLOOR
OF THE CASA MILÀ
→
THE IMPOSING UNDULATING
FACADE OF THE CASA MILÀ
SUGGESTS THE LIFE AND
MOVEMENT OF THE STONE

P. 142-143
→
THE RAILS ON THE BALCONIES,
AUTHENTIC IRON SCULPTURES,
WERE CREATED BY JUJOL
USING THE FIRST ONE AS A
MODEL, WHICH WAS DESIGNED
AND EVEN CAST BY GAUDÍ
HIMSELF

P. 144-145
→
THE CAST IRON DOORS
COVER THE ENTRANCE LIKE
SPIDERS' WEBS
→
THE STRUCTURE OF LA
PEDRERA IS OPEN PLAN, AN
ARCHITECTURAL SOLUTION
WITH WHICH THE BUILDING IS
SUPPORTED BY COLUMNS,
FREEING THE FACADES FROM
THE LOAD

→
THE ENTRANCE LOBBY
IN PASSEIG DE GRÀCIA

P. 148-149
→
GAUDÍ USES THE COURTYARDS
AS THE CENTRAL AXIS OF THE
BUILDING
→
JUST LIKE AN INVERTED KEEL
OF A BOAT, THE SERIES OF
OVERHEAD ARCHES IN BRICK
SUPPORT THE WEIGHT OF
THE TERRACE ROOF

P. 150-151
→→
THE BUILDING'S ROOF
RECREATES AN ONEIRIC AND
SUGGESTIVE WORLD WHERE
CHIMNEYS AND VENTILATION
DUCTS ARE TRANSFORMED
INTO DISTURBING
ANTHROMORPHIC SHAPES

P. 152-153
→
THE FLAT ROOF OF THE CASA
MILÀ SYNTHESISES AND
PERFECTS THE TREATMENT
THAT GAUDÍ GAVE TO ALL
THE CROWNING ELEMENTS
THROUGHOUT THE WORK

CRYPT OF THE GÜELL INDUSTRIAL VILLAGE

Eusebi Güell established an industrial village in Santa Coloma de Cervelló. Gaudí should have erected a new church but finally only the crypt was completed.

The architect, who had begun the project in 1898, abandoned the directorship of the works in 1914. The entire work is possibly Gaudí's great masterpiece as regards the overcoming of complexity and its unusualness "per se".

→
THE CERAMIC ORNAMENTS
REPRESENT CHRISTIAN
SYMBOLS SUCH AS THE CROSS,
THE FISH AND THE LETTERS
ALPHA (BEGINNING) AND
OMEGA (END)
→
THE GENERAL IRREGULAR FORM
OF THE CRYPT IS DUE TO THE
PRESSURE FROM THE LAND.
THE LEANING COLUMNS ARE
OF BASALT, BRICK AND STONE

P. 158-159
→
THE ARCHITECTURE
HARMONISES WITH THE
NATURAL ENVIRONMENT THAT
GAUDÍ RESPECTED, EVEN
CHANGING THE SHAPE OF THE
STAIRWAY IN ORDER TO SAVE A
TREE: "I CAN MAKE A STAIRWAY
IN 3 WEEKS BUT IT TAKES 20
YEARS TO MAKE A PINE TREE"

P. 160-161
→
THE CRYPT IS CHARACTERISED
BY THE HYPERBOLOID ROOF,
THE PARABOLIC ARCHES AND
THE CATALAN-STYLE VAULTING.
IN THE PICTURE, THE
MONOGRAM OF CHRIST
→
THE CURRENT STAINED-GLASS
WINDOWS, WHOSE FORM
REMINDS ONE OF FLOWER
PETALS OR BUTTERFLY WINGS,
ARE A COPY OF THE ORIGINALS
THAT WERE DESTROYED IN 1936

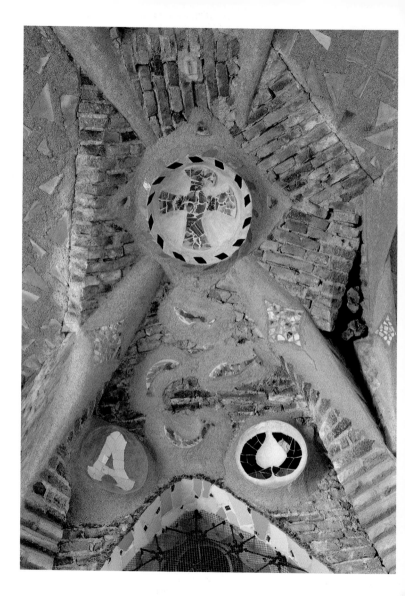

THE FINAL YEARS (1914-1926)

In the Nerja cave (Málaga), the guide shows visitors an inverted "Sagrada Família" that hangs from the ceiling. They are Gaudí's catenaries, something the guide is not aware of. What he is also unaware of is that in the Sagrada Família, particularly on the portal of the Nativity, with its four spire bell towers, although the form is very important, it is not the most important aspect. Neither is the fact that it is integrated into nature and the architecture "lives" within the geological aspect of the work. What overshadows all this is the feeling of supernatural grandeur that invigorates each stone and which makes Gaudí not only a prodigious "inventor" within 20th century art styles, but also the last cathedral builder, the genius who closed, not so much a period in time, but more an entire world, a world whose beginnings we were unable to chart from this or that Gothic or Romanesque cathedral but, for its virgin power, perhaps, can be dated in the megalithic ring at Stonehenge. The texture, matter, form, light, reality and movement in Gaudí's Sagrada Família speak of a struggle and a triumph which can really not be explained, as has been said before, without referring to the supernatural. If the human power of sublimation and transformation has ever been seen in a given world in rising ascendancy – made from raw material – then it is in the Sagrada Família. The crypt is quite extraordinary with its solution of the apse pinnacles, as is the highly interesting ornamentation on the facade of the Nativity, with its peculiar softened underwater Baroque, a polyform of abstractions converted into volumi-

←
MODEL OF THE CRYPT
OF THE CHURCH OF
THE GÜELL INDUSTRIAL
VILLAGE

nous space, of impulses transformed into shapes and with naturalistic inserts (plaster living sculptures hollowed out). None of these aspects can be compared, in our opinion, with the mystical and magical terrifying violence that the group of four parabolic bell towers possesses. These penetrative towers, simultaneously reaching to and being pulled towards the heavens represent the overcoming of a worldly human existence. The same polychrome at the tops, which we have mentioned before, is not superior to the dry harshness and stony texture of the towers that gradually thin out, making us climb with their own impetus. It is understood that Gaudí, who discovered, precisely on the project for this portal, the secret of its most prized shape and its perfect structure, wanted to devote himself entirely to this work in the twelve years before his death, before a fatal accident put an end to something that was never finished.

This feeling of infinity, more than that of being unfinished, reigns over the total creation of the Sagrada Família, particularly in the concept of its whole – loaded with the complex symbolism of the "temple-mountain" and of the "cavern" –. The model of the temple, the projects drawn by Gaudí, with the solutions for the roofing, as well as the models of specific elements, such as the elliptical windows inserted into triangles or in bony crystallisations, are the demonstration of a spirit which, instead of feeling fear from this infinity, was in fact in its true element. For Gaudí, the Sagrada Família represented the passing of Gothic architecture, not only for the elimination of the flying buttresses and buttresses or for the metamorpho-

THE ORIGINALITY AND
SIMPLICITY OF THE
SAGRADA FAMÍLIA
SCHOOLS IMPRESSED
LE CORBUSIER GREATLY

sis of its "ornamental structures", but also for the total conversion of its entire system, creating a new geometry, eliminating to a large extent that which was discontinuous or making the discontinuous into a continuous effect – as is seen by the simple comparison between a bell tower of the temple with gothic spires –. He was thus able to, with an irrefutable intensification of the irrational, or rather, of the super-rational, achieve what had seemed impossible to further: the ascendant rising that is judged as the essence of Faustian-Gothic. The work described in drawings by Gaudí, the unfinished work, like an immense score that no orchestra on earth would have been capable of performing, could be an enigma for future generations concerning its completion. Alternatively, it could be judged as perfectly well defined and without problems. Nevertheless, whatever the case, it is one of the architect's richest, most subtle and powerful manifestations which brought down the "traditional" system in the dawning of a world which, for its selfsame differential feeling, was forced to understand him and give him the credit that his own period unjustly and unwholesomely negated to a large extent.

To say before Gaudí's work that he was a genius of expression but question whether this quality helped him as an architect; to list, in going against such an adverse thesis, that he was the first European constructor to understand the possibilities of reinforced concrete; to say that he was the precursor of garden city urban planning; that he created, with his increased appreciation of a craftsman's technique – vaulting *a la Catalan* – and is the direct precedent to shell vaulting so much used today by Candela, among others; to mention his incorporation of artisan skills into architecture, etc.; to even quote him as a formal source of the expressionism of Poelzig, Steiner and Mendelsohn all seems naïve compared to what has emerged from our passionate tale. The heresy of today's architecture is perhaps in only seeing certain "conditions" that are judged as strictly architectural, evaluating everything from a social or economic point of view, or from a technical one. Gaudí is the Michelangelo of a much more heartrending, complex and contradictory era than that of the 16th century. Not only is he the creator of a morphological universe applying the corresponding mechanical laws; he is also the absolute intellectual predecessor of the modern sculptural world and even the inspirer of a large part of "material" painting. However, far and above these artistic values, as well as the architectural values we have already mentioned, is the secret violence and sacred strength of his soul, shown in works that exist and are part of the history of mankind.

→
DRAWING BY GAUDÍ OF THE
PORTAL OF THE PASSION
→
HUMAN FIGURE
SURROUNDED BY MIRRORS
TO OBTAIN DIFFERENT
PERSPECTIVES

TEMPLE DE
LA SAGRADA FAMÍLIA

Construction work began on the Sagrada Família in 1882. Its promoter, Josep Bocabella, entrusted the work to the architect Francisco de Paula del Villar who, in 1883, was replaced by Gaudí. From this moment on, the work on the temple would accompany him for the rest of his life and he introduced architectural solutions that he had tested and solved in other projects. The temple, that would be called the "Cathedral of the Poor", had to be financed entirely by donations. The works continue up to this day, following the plans that the architect left behind.

→
IN 1892 GAUDÍ BEGAN THE
FACADE OF THE NATIVITY
ON THE 30TH OF NOVEMBER
1925 THE FIRST BELL TOWER,
DEDICATED TO ST. BARNABUS,
WAS COMPLETED. GAUDÍ
SPOKE OF HIS PLEASURE OF
SEEING "HOW THAT SPEAR
JOINS HEAVEN AND EARTH"
→
THE NATIVITY GROUP BY
JAUME BUSQUETS WHICH
IS CURRENTLY SURROUNDED
BY THE ANGELS BY THE
JAPANESE SCULPTOR
ETSURO SOTOO

P. 172-173
→
THE TRUMPETER ANGELS
BY THE SCULPTOR LLORENÇ
MATAMALA WERE PLACED
IN 1899
→
THE FOUR BELL TOWERS ON
THE FACADE OF THE NATIVITY
WERE COMPLETED IN 1930

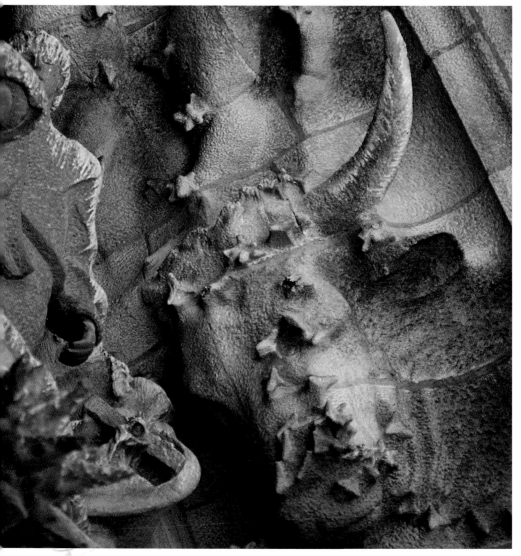

P. 174-175

←
THE TORTOISE, A SYMBOLIC
ANIMAL OVER WHICH THE
UNIVERSE IS SUPPORTED,
IS AT THE FOOT OF THE
COLUMNS OF THE FACADE
OF THE NATIVITY

←
REPRESENTATION OF THE
ZODIACAL SIGN OF TAURUS

→
SNAIL ON ONE OF THE APSE
CORNERS

→
THE DIZZY SPIRAL OF THE
STEPS ON THE INSIDE OF
THE TOWERS IS FASCINATING
AS IT TAKES US INTO THE
INSIDE OF A GIGANTIC STONE
SNAIL

→
OVER THE GROUND PLAN THAT
WAS STARTED BY FRANCISCO
DE PAULA DEL VILLAR, GAUDÍ
COMPLETED THE CRYPT
→
VAULTING KEYSTONE IN
THE CRYPT WITH THE
REPRESENTATION OF THE
ANNUNCIATION OF MARY
BY THE SCULPTOR FLOTATS

IN 1899 THE CHAPEL IN THE CLOISTER OF THE VIRGIN OF THE ROSARY WAS COMPLETED AND ON WHICH GAUDÍ WORKED WITH EXTREME EXACTITUDE ON THE DETAILS

REPRESENTATION OF ALLEGORIES IN THE CHAPEL OF THE ROSARY:

VANITY, WOMAN'S TEMPTATION

VIOLENCE AND MAN'S TEMPTATION

FILIGREE THAT REMINDS ONE OF LACEWORK AND BASKETWORK

THE ANGEL PLAYING WITH FOAM ON THE VAULTING KEYSTONE

→
EN 1911 GAUDÍ BECAME ILL
WITH MALTESE FEVER AND
FROM HIS CONVALESCENCE
IN PUIGCERDÀ HE IMAGINED
THE FACADE OF THE PASSION
"I AM PREPARED TO SACRIFICE
THE VERY CONSTRUCTION,
TO BREAK VAULTING AND CUT
COLUMNS TO GIVE AN IDEA
OF HOW CRUEL SACRIFICE IS"
→
IN 1990, IN THE ATRIUM OF
THE FACADE OF THE PASSION,
THE FIRST SCULPTURES
ENTRUSTED TO JOSEP MARIA
SUBIRACHS WERE POSITIONED

→
PINNACLE BY THE SCULPTOR
ETSURO SOTOO
  →
THE INTERSECTION OF THE
HYPERBOLOIDS OF THE
VAULTING FORM STARRED
POLYGONS

P. 186-187
→
THE NAVE REPRODUCES THE
IDEA OF THE FOREST OF
COLUMNS, SOME OF WHICH
REACH 21 METRES IN HEIGHT
AS THE TREES BRANCH OFF
ON REACHING THE VAULTING

BIOGRAPHICAL NOTES ON GAUDI

1852 25th of June, born in Reus. Fifth and youngest son of a craftsman boilermaker.

1863 He entered the college of the Piarist Fathers to complete his secondary education.

1865 In this year he produced drawings for the magazine "El Arlequín". He became a friend of Toda, with whom he collaborated on a reconstruction project on the monastery of Poblet (partially destroyed in 1835). First demonstrations of his love for nature and medieval art.

1869 He moved to Barcelona, to study his final year of secondary education. His father accompanied him and closed the workshop in Reus. His other son, Francisco, finished his medical studies in this year.

1872 He entered the Senior School of Architecture of Barcelona.

1876 There remain notes of this year written by Gaudí in a "diary". His brother, Francisco, died some time between 1873 and 1876. His father had to sell the land he owned in order to pay for his son's architectural studies. Gaudí took a special interest in the philosophy and literature classes of Francesc Llorens i Barba and those of art history given by Pau Milà i Fontanals. Gaudí worked with the architect Francisco de Paula del Villar in works on the sanctuary of Montserrat (the jewel room of the statue of the Virgin). He also worked with the architect Josep Fontseré on the decoration of the Cuitadella Park in Barcelona (the wrought-iron railings on the entrance, the aquarium medallions on the waterfall). During these years, he also worked with the architect Joan Martorell Montells, a very religious man with strong ideas about social reform.

1878 On the 15th of March he attained the qualification of architect. He met Eusebi Güell, who was to be his main client and sponsor.

1878-1882 The "Mataró Industrial Village". He placed the stairway on the outside of the building and at the side, as Gropius would do in 1914, in the Werkbund factory in Cologne. He only built the factory, whose machine room (which survives today) shows a parabolic structure in the framework. The biographies about Gaudí in this period tell of his unsuccessful love affair, which may have determined his deep psychological change.

1883 The chapel project for the Alella parish church.

1883 He was named as architect for the Sagrada Família cathedral. In 1869 an administrative board had been set up for the works on the Expiatory Temple and in 1882 the first stone of the project was laid by de Francisco de Paula del Villar. On renouncing the project, Juan Martorell was proposed and he in turn rejected the post in favour of Gaudí, who at that time was 31 years old.

1883-1888 The Casa Vicens, Barcelona. It shows the Mudejar influence. Adequate and abundant use of glazed ceramic tiling and iron. Colour.

1883-1885 "El Capricho" in Comillas (Santander), a work in which aspects of the Casa Vicens were accentuated and dramatised, maintaining the Mudejar influence.

1884-1887 The crypt of the Sagrada Família cathedral, whose walls had been built by Villar according to his neo-gothic project and which Gaudí modified with his naturalist-expressionist morphologist approach.

1884-1888 An intensive period of working for Eusebi Güell that included the Güell Pavilions in Pedralbes, which signalled the crisis for Gaudian Mudejar style work. An important wrought iron gate, "The Dragon". Construction of the Güell Palace in Carrer Nou de la Rambla in Barcelona. Widespread use of parabolic forms and of a fragmented but monumental space. The appearance of chimneys of a sculptural nature and geometric forms with a certain magical content. In the main room, paintings by Aleix Clapés (1850-1920). Portals of a funicular structure.

1888-1890 Theresan College in Carrer Ganduxer in Barcelona, a work begun by another architect. An austere work produced in brick and rustic stone. Its expression is based on a rhythm of parabolic arches against a monumental surface. A certain Mudejar style persists. Interior galleries with parabolic arches.

1889-1893 First constructive stage of the Episcopal Palace in Astorga (León), which was interrupted until 1907. A work in granite, sober. Use of ceramics in the decoration of the second floor.

1891-1892 The "Los Botines" project, a building in León, which was entrusted to him by clients of Eusebi Güell. A work produced within a fairly impersonal style that was begun in 1892. Above the portal, however, appears an image of St. George (the first example of sculpture by Gaudí in his constructions).

1891-1893 Construction of the apse in the Sagrada Família in Barcelona. He maintained a great part of the neo-gothic style but transformed it with new imagination and feeling. The facade depicting the Nativity was started.

1892 The project for the building of the Catholic Missions in Tangier. The spindle-shaped bell towers appear, which would later define the Sagrada Família, an element of probable African origin. There is a curious relationship between this element and the Hamite buildings (Kreis Següela, northern Togo). The project for the Catholic Missions in Tangier was almost certainly influenced by a trip to Morocco.

1898-1900 The Casa Calvet en Barcelona. Building in carved stone, in which the dominating factor is the containment. Undulating top outline finished in spherical pinnacles. The attic balconies are of perforated cast iron plate, prefiguring those of the Casa Batlló. Gaudí, in this case as in others before for the Casa Vicens, the Comillas chapel and the Güell palace, designed the furnishings in a deeply personal way. In the same year he began the studies for the church at the Güell Industrial Village in Santa Coloma de Cervelló (Barcelona). The studies continued for ten years and it was not until 1908 when work finally started on the crypt.

1900-1909 Bellesguard Building. Deeply personal and expressionist stylisation of Gothic. Built in schistose rock. Catalan-style vaulting. The use of wrought iron work. In the same period and similar to Miralles (stone and iron wall, whose rhythm is connected to that of the future bench of Park Güell).

1900 Gaudí worked on Park Güell and resided in the chalet with his aged father and niece Rosa Egea Gaudí (who died in 1906 and 1912 respectively). Park Güell is a large urban area situated on the Muntanya Pelada, in an area covering 15 hectares.

1900-1903 Construction of the main buildings of Park Güell: walls, main stairway, pavilions, etc. Here there is a marked contrast of expression, rather than style, between different elements of this park. To the imaginative, lyrical and chromatic nature of the pavilions and main stairway is the contrast of the dramatic and sullen aspect of the leaning portico arches in a tawny colour. A curvilinear, snake-like rhythm dominates the work. By means of the leaning columns is the application of a mechanical principle (column in the direction of the force line determined by the load) in order to provide an aesthetic effect, which also appears in the crypt of the church of the Güell Industrial Village.

1904-1914 Restoration works on the cathedral of Majorca. Very respectful work with this medieval construction in which the stained glass windows and wrought iron work are of special note, as well as the ceramic work realised by his assistant Jujol.

1904-1907 Casa Batlló. Some Gaudí historians date the beginning of this work in 1902. It is the remodelling of an already standing building in Passeig de Gràcia in Barcelona. An extraordinarily beautiful chromatic facade, which has been defined as a "surface made of vertical water" and has an unmistakable similarity with Monet's Nymphettes. The colour has a deforming effect. The roofing has a scale-like finish that reminds one of the back of a prehistoric monster. The iron balconies are of great sculptural value. The fantasy-like chimneys are more advanced than those in the Güell palace. Indisputable involvement of Jujol, to whom it seems the roof collages in the hypostyle hall of Park Güell are attributed. On the inside the forms show Gaudí's new morphology. The use of wood. Furnishing designed by Gaudí.

1906-1912 Casa Milà. Revolutionary use of an expressionist form, in stone, in the Eixample district of Barcelona. Building of interior walls. Undulating facades. White attic in curvilinear slope. Chimneys and other structures over the roof, showing the more extensive development of these elements in Gaudí's work, with a deep magical sense and approaching the world of Ernst, in terms of sense, and Moore in terms of structure. Helicoid forms. Dynamic-linear rhythm on the wrought iron work on the balcony parapets. Collaboration with Rubió, Jujol, Bayó and Canaleta. Paintings by Aleix Clapés in the vestibules. Parabolic arch curvature in the attic. It has been said that Gaudí projected the building as a pedestal of a monument to the Virgin, by means of a series by the expressionist sculptor Carlos Mani (1866-1911), which was destroyed.

1910-1912 The bench in Park Güell of a double undulating rhythm in raised and levelled contour. Decorated with broken tiles that form abstract compositions in colour, exactly coeval with the early non-figurative paintings by Kandinsky.

1908-1914 Construction of the crypt of the church at the Güell Industrial Village, in Santa Coloma de Cervelló. Hyperboloid roof. Parabolic arches and Catalan-style vaulting. Extraordinarily original stained glass windows which contribute to creating the space. In the model of the church of the Güell Industrial Village, the overhead structures were made for the study of loads and forms, in collaboration with Francesc Berenguer. The general irregular form of the crypt is determined by the force of the land. Leaning columns in basalt, brick and stone. Ceramic ornamental motifs.

1914-1926 Exclusive devotion to the temple of the Sagrada Família. Construction of the spindle-shaped bell towers whose finishes remind one of the colours of the underwater flora and fauna in the painting of Gustav Klimt. Naturalist sculpture, with plaster spaces over life models on the facade of the Nativity. These years are the years of Gaudí's solitary lifestyle and his detachment from anything irreverent. On the 7th of June 1926 he is run over by a tram, an accident that caused his death.

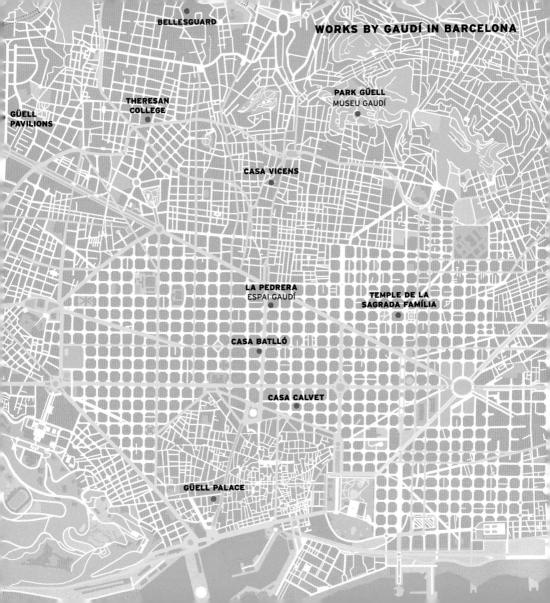

WORKS BY GAUDÍ IN BARCELONA

BELLESGUARD

GÜELL
PAVILIONS

THERESAN
COLLEGE

PARK GÜELL
MUSEU GAUDÍ

CASA VICENS

LA PEDRERA
ESPAI GAUDÍ

TEMPLE DE LA
SAGRADA FAMÍLIA

CASA BATLLÓ

CASA CALVET

GÜELL PALACE

ORIGINAL TEXT
Lourdes and Victoria Cirlot

© PHOTOGRAPHY
Pere Vivas, Ricard Pla
Jordi Puig / Pere Vivas, p. 118, 120, 121.
Juanjo Puente / Pere Vivas, p. 94, 186
Robert Justamante, p. 36, 37.

COMPLEMENTARY TEXTS
Antonio G. Funes

ACKNOWLEDGEMENTS
Institut Municipal de Parcs i Jardins, Barcelona.
Fundació Caixa Catalunya, Casa Batlló, Casa Bellesguard,
Casa Vicens, Junta Constructora del Temple Expiatori
de la Sagrada Família.
Josep Mª Carandell, germans Gascón (Museu Gaudí),
Juan-José Lahuerta, Jaume Rosell.

DESIGN
Joan Colomer

TRANSLATION
Steve Cedar

COLOUR SEPARATIONS
Tecnoart

PRINTED BY
NG Nivell Gràfic, Barcelona
03/2006

DEPÓSITO LEGAL
B. 12.518 - 2001

ISBN
84-89815-94-1